Active Second Edition
LISTENING

STEVEN BROWN

DOROLYN SMITH

CAMBRIDGE UNIVERSITY PRESS
Cambridge, New York, Melbourne, Madrid, Cape Town, Singapore, São Paulo

Cambridge University Press
32 Avenue of the Americas, New York, NY 10013-2473

www.cambridge.org
Information on this title: www.cambridge.org/9780521678179

© Cambridge University Press 2007

First published 2007

Printed in Hong Kong, China, by Golden Cup Printing Company, Limited

A catalog record for this book is available from the British Library

ISBN-13 978-0-521-67817-9 student's book and self-study audio CD
ISBN-10 0-521-67817-X student's book and self-study audio CD

ISBN-13 978-0-521-67818-6 teacher's manual and audio CD
ISBN-10 0-521-67818-8 teacher's manual and audio CD

ISBN-13 978-0-521-67819-3 CDs (audio)
ISBN-10 0-521-67819-6 CDs (audio)

Art direction, book design, photo research, and layout services: Adventure House, NYC
Audio production: Full House, NYC

Contents

Plan of the book

Acknowledgments

Text credits

52 Courtesy of Campbell Soup Company

52 Häagen-Dazs® is a registered trademark of General Mills, Inc., and is used with permission.

52 Used with permission from McDonald's Corporation.

Illustration credits

Jessica Allen: 47
CB Canga: 72, 73
Andrea Cobb: 68
James Elston: 6, 24, 25, 43, 61
Chuck Gonzales: 5, 8, 19, 38, 55

Ben Kirchner: 18, 27, 66, 78
Joe Le Monnier: 10–11
Frank Montagna: 9, 13, 28, 39, 51, 71, 75
Terry Wong: 20, 30, 36
Filip Yip: 4, 29, 54, 56

Photography credits

3 © Superstock

7 © Alamy

12 (*clockwise from top left*) © Hugh Sitton/ Punchstock; © Jupiter Images; © Bob Krist/ Corbis; © Steve Allen Travel Photography/Alamy; © Punchstock; © Roger Wood/Corbis

16 (*left to right*) © Punchstock; © Galen Rowell/ Corbis

22 (*clockwise from top left*) © Frans Lemmens/ Corbis; © Visual Israel/StockFood America; © Age fotostock; © Rick Strange/Newscom; © Dave Mckay/Alamy

23 © Doug McKinlay/Lonely Planet Images

26 (*clockwise from top left*) © Bureau L.A. Collection/Corbis; © Everett Collection; © Warner Brothers/Everett Collection; © Walt Disney Pictures/Newscom; © 20th Century Fox/Everett Collection; © Columbia/Everett Collection

32–33 © Peter Pioppo

34 (*clockwise from top left*) © Chris Everard/Getty Images; © Rick Souders/Jupiter Images; © Allison Dinner/Getty Images; © Istock

37 (*first row, left to right*) © Todd Gipstein/Getty Images; © Getty Images; © Punchstock; © Oliver Lang/Getty Images; (*second row, left to right*) © Istock; © Getty Images; © Punchstock; (*third row, left to right*) © Steve Fitchett/Getty Images; © Getty Images; © Punchstock; © Corbis; (*fourth row, left to right*) © Punchstock; © Punchstock; © Photos.com

40 (*clockwise from top left*) © Lucid Images/Age fotostock; © Alamy; © Alamy; © Punchstock; © Stuart Pearce/Age fotostock

44 (*top row, left to right*) © NBC/Everett Collection; © ABC/Everett Collection; (*middle*) © AP Wide World; (*bottom row, left to right*) © Fred Prouser/ Reuters/Newscom; © Shizuo Kambayashi/AP Wide World; (*TV*) © Alamy

46 © Getty Images

48 (*clockwise from top left*) © Alamy; © Robert Holmes/Alamy; © Robert Holmes/Corbis; © Punchstock; © Alamy

50 (*top row, left to right*) © Punchstock; © Brian Hagiwara/Jupiter Images; © Maximilian Stock/ StockFood America; (*middle row, left to right*) © Getty Images; © Getty Images; © Photo Japan/Alamy; (*bottom row, left to right*) © Jupiter Images; © Jupiter Images; © Photos.com

52 (*clockwise from top left*) © AP Wide World; © IML Image Group/Alamy; © Scott Olson/ Getty Images; © Andre Jenny/Alamy

58 © Fridmar Damm/Corbis

59 (*clockwise from top left*) © Juergen Hasenkopf/ Alamy; © Fotosearch; © Alamy; © Charles & Josette Lenars/Corbis; © Alamy

60 (*clockwise from top right*) © Jupiter Images; © Jupiter Images; © Punchstock; © Punchstock; © Jupiter Images

62 © Age fotostock

65 (*clockwise from top left*) © Joe McBride/Corbis; © Punchstock; © Robert Holmes/Corbis; © Mark E. Gibson/Corbis; © Punchstock; © Gail Mooney/Corbis

69 (*left to right*) © Corbis; © Bob Handelman/Alamy

70 (*clockwise from top left*) © Lise Aserud/AFP/ Newscom; © Barbara Peacock/Getty Images; © Bob Birch/Index Stock; © Yoshikazu Tsuno/ AFP/Newscom; © Tina Manley/Alamy; © AP Wide World

74 © Shutter Stock

76 © Punchstock

77 (*all*) © Punchstock

Author acknowledgments

We would like to thank our **reviewers** for their helpful suggestions:
Andrew Newton, **Sogang University**, Seoul, South Korea
Yao-feng Huang, **Tajen University**, Pingtung, Taiwan
Gordon Sites, **Keihoku Junior High School**, Chiba, Japan
Brooks Slaybaugh, **Tamagawa Gakuen**, Tokyo, Japan
David Philip, **Pusan National University**, Pusan, South Korea
Robert Bendergrass, **Pukyong National University**, Pusan, South Korea

We would also like to acknowledge the **students** and **teachers** in the following schools and institutes
who piloted components of the first edition of *Active Listening*:

Alianza Cultural Uruguay-Estados Unidos, Montevideo, Uruguay; **Bae Centre**, Buenos Aires,
Argentina; **Bunka Institute of Foreign Languages**, Tokyo, Japan; **Educational Options**, Santa Clara,
California, U.S.A.; **Impact English**, Santiago, Chile; **Instituto Cultural de Idiomas Ltda.**, Caxias do
Sul, Brazil; **Kansai University of Foreign Studies**, Osaka, Japan; **Koyo Choji Co. Ltd.**, Hitachi, Japan;
National Chin-Yi Institute of Technology, Taichung, Taiwan; **Osaka Institute of Technology**, Osaka,
Japan; **Southern Illinois University**, Niigata, Japan; **Suzugamine Women's College**, Hiroshima City,
Japan; **Tokyo Foreign Language College**, Tokyo, Japan; **Umeda Business College**, Osaka, Japan;
University of Michigan English Language Institute, Ann Arbor, Michigan, U.S.A.

Thanks also go to those **interviewed** for the **Expansion** units: Bahija Jari, Seng Yeow Lee, Mariann
Novak, Bill Wheeler, and to the English Language Institute at the University of Pittsburgh for support
during this project.

A special thanks to the **editorial** and **production** team at Cambridge University Press who worked on
this edition:
Eleanor Barnes, David Bohlke, Karen Brock, Rob Freire, Deborah Goldblatt, Yuri Hara, Louisa
Hellegers, Lise Minovitz, Sandra Pike, Danielle Power, Tami Savir, Jaimie Scanlon, Kayo Taguchi,
Louisa van Houten, and Dorothy Zemach. This book is much better because of their careful work and
helpful insights.

Thanks to the Cambridge University Press **staff** and **advisors**:
Harry Ahn, Yumiko Akeba, Michelle Kim, Andy Martin, Nigel McQuitty, Carine Mitchell, Mark
O'Neil, Rebecca Ou, Bruno Paul, Dan Schulte, Catherine Shih, Howard Siegelman, and Ivan Sorrentino.

Very special thanks to Deborah Goldblatt, who has been enthusiastic about this project for longer than
she would have preferred. Thanks for her patience and her support over the years.

Finally, we would like to acknowledge and thank Marc Helgesen for his role as author on the first
edition. He's remained a great friend and source of ideas throughout the writing of this book.

To the teacher

Active Listening, Second Edition is a fully updated and revised edition of the popular three-level listening series for adult and young adult learners of North American English. Each level offers students 16 engaging, task-based units, each built around a topic, function, or grammatical theme. Grounded in the theory that learners are more successful listeners when they activate their prior knowledge of a topic, the series gives students a frame of reference to make predictions about what they will hear. Through a careful balance of activities, students learn to listen for main ideas, to listen for details, and to listen and make inferences.

Active Listening, Second Edition Level 2 is intended for low-intermediate to intermediate students. It can be used as a main text for listening classes or as a component in speaking or integrated-skills classes.

The second edition differs from the first in a number of ways. In recent years, there has been a greater emphasis on the role of vocabulary and pronunciation in the field of second language acquisition. To reflect this emphasis, the second edition provides a more refined vocabulary syllabus and a more extensive preview of words. The final section of each unit has also been expanded to provide a full-page speaking activity, including pronunciation practice. In addition, the Listening tasks in each unit have been expanded. Students listen to the same input twice, each time listening for a different purpose and focusing on a listening skill appropriate for that purpose. Other changes in the second edition include the systematic integration of cultural information. Most units contain interesting cultural information in the listening tasks, and a new, two-page Expansion unit, containing cultural information about a country or region of the world and an authentic student interview, has been added after every four units to review and extend the language and topics of the previous units. Each unit also has a Self-study page, accompanied by an audio CD, that can be used for self-study or for homework.

ABOUT THE BOOK

The book includes 16 core units and four expansion units. Each core unit has four parts: **Warming up**, two main **Listening tasks**, and **Your turn to talk**, a speaking activity for pairs or small groups. The four **Expansion** units present cultural information related to the unit themes. In addition, there is an introductory lesson called **Before you begin**. This lesson introduces students to helpful learning strategies and types of listening.

The units can be taught in the order presented or out of sequence to follow the themes of the class or another book it is supplementing. In general, the tasks in the second half of the book are more challenging than those in the first, and language from earlier units is recycled as the book progresses.

Unit organization

Each unit begins with an activity called **Warming up**. This activity, usually done in pairs, serves two purposes: It reminds students of what they already know about the topic, and it previews common vocabulary used in the unit. When they do the warming up activity, students use their prior knowledge, or "schema," about the topic, vocabulary, and structures, as well as learn new vocabulary and phrases that are connected to the theme of the unit. The combination of the two approaches makes the listening tasks that follow easier.

Listening task 1 and **Listening task 2** are the major listening exercises. Each task has two parts. The students work with the same input in both parts of the task, but they listen for different reasons each time. The tasks are balanced to include a variety of listening skills, which are identified in a box to the left of each listening exercise. Because *Active Listening* features a task-based approach, students should do the activities as they listen, rather than wait until they have finished listening to a particular segment. To make this easier, writing is kept to a minimum. In most cases, students check boxes, number items, circle answers, or write only words or short phrases.

Your turn to talk, the final section of each unit, is a short, fluency-oriented speaking task done in pairs or small groups. First, students *prepare* for the speaking activity by gathering ideas and thinking about the topic. Next, they *practice* a pronunciation point. Finally, they *speak* to their classmates as they exchange information or opinions.

The two-page **Expansion** unit after every four units features listening activities that provide general cultural information about a country or region of the world and an authentic interview with a person from that place. The tasks focus on the same listening skills as the core units and recycle the themes and topics of the preceding four units.

The **Self-study** page reviews language, vocabulary, and themes from the unit and provides personalization exercises. It can be used for homework or for additional listening practice in class.

Hints and techniques

- Be sure to do the **Warming up** section for each unit. This preview can help students develop useful learning strategies. It also helps students to be more successful listeners, which, in turn, motivates and encourages them.

- Try to play a particular segment only one or two times. If students are still having difficulty, try telling them the answers. Then play the audio again and let them experience understanding what they heard previously.

- If some students find listening very difficult, have them do the task in pairs, helping each other as necessary. The **Teacher's Manual,** described in the box in the next column, contains additional ideas.

- Some students may not be used to active learning. Those students may be confused by your instructions, since they are used to a more passive role. Explaining activities verbally is usually the least effective way to give instructions. It is better to demonstrate. For example, read the instructions as briefly as possible (e.g., "Listen. Number the

pictures."). Then play the first part of the audio program. Stop the recording and elicit the correct answer from the students. Those who weren't sure what to do will quickly understand. The same techniques work for **Warming up** and **Your turn to talk.** Lead one pair or group through the first step of the task. As the other students watch, they will quickly see what they are supposed to do.

Active Listening, Second Edition Level 2 is accompanied by a Teacher's Manual that contains step-by-step teaching notes with key words highlighted, optional speaking activities and listening strategies, photocopiable unit quizzes for each Student's Book unit, and two complete photocopiable tests with audio CD.

HOW STUDENTS LEARN TO LISTEN

Many students find listening to be one of the most difficult skills in English. The following explains some of the ideas incorporated into the book to make students become more effective listeners. *Active Listening, Second Edition* Level 2 is designed to help students make real and rapid progress. Recent research into teaching listening and its related receptive skill, reading, has given insights into how successful students learn foreign or second languages.

Bottom-up vs. top-down processing: a brick-wall analogy

To understand what our students are going through as they learn to listen or read, consider the "bottom-up vs. top-down processing" distinction. The distinction is based on the ways students process and attempt to understand what they read or hear. With bottom-up processing, students start with the component parts: words, grammar, and the like. Top-down processing is the opposite. Students start from their background knowledge.

This might be better understood by means of a metaphor. Imagine a brick wall. If you are standing at the bottom looking at the wall brick by brick, you can easily see the details. It is difficult, however, to get an overall view of the wall. And, if you come to a missing brick (e.g., an unknown word or unfamiliar structure), you're stuck. If, on the other hand, you're sitting on the top of the wall, you can easily see the landscape. Of course, because of distance, you'll miss some details.

Students, particularly those with years of "classroom English" but little experience in really using the language, try to listen from the "bottom up."

They attempt to piece the meaning together, word by word. It is difficult for us, as native and advanced non-native English users, to experience what students go through. However, try reading the following *from right to left.*

> word one ,slowly English process you When to easy is it ,now doing are you as ,time a at .word individual each of meaning the catch understand to difficult very is it ,However .passage the of meaning overall the

You were probably able to understand the paragraph:

> When you process English slowly, one word at a time, as you are doing now, it is easy to catch the meaning of each individual word. However, it is very difficult to understand the overall meaning of the passage.

While reading, however, it is likely you felt the frustration of bottom-up processing; you had to get each individual part before you could make sense of it. This is similar to what our students experience – and they're having to wrestle the meaning in a foreign language. Of course, this is an ineffective way to listen since it takes too long. While students are still trying to make sense of what has been said, the speaker keeps going. The students get lost.

Although their processing strategy makes listening difficult, students do come to class with certain strengths. From their years of English study, most have a relatively large, if passive, vocabulary. They also often have a solid receptive knowledge of English grammar. We shouldn't neglect the years of life experience; our students bring with them a wealth of background knowledge on many topics. These three strengths – vocabulary, grammar, and life experience – can be the tools for effective listening.

The **Warming up** activities in *Active Listening* build on those strengths. By engaging the students in active, meaningful prelistening tasks, students integrate bottom-up and top-down processing. They start from meaning, but, in the process of doing the task, use vocabulary and structures (grammar) connected with the task, topic, or function. The result is an integrated listening strategy.

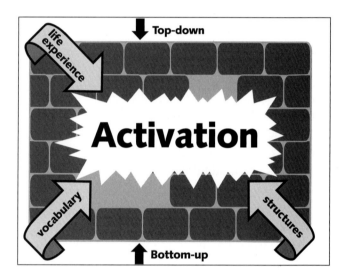

Types of listening

A second factor that is essential in creating effective listeners is exposing them to a variety of types of listening. Many students have only had experience with listening for literal comprehension. While listening for details, or specific information, is an important skill, it represents only one type. We have attempted to reach a balance in the book in order to give students experience with – and an understanding of – listening for the main idea, or gist, and listening and making inferences. Students usually are quick to understand the idea of listening for the main idea. They can easily imagine having to catch the general meaning of something they hear. Inference – listening "between the lines" – can be more difficult.

Take the following examples (from the introductory unit, **Before you begin**). The students hear the following conversation:

Man: I love this store! They have the best prices.
Woman: Me, too. I always spend too much money here.
Man: I think I'm going to buy this computer for school.
Woman: Wow! That's nice. How much is it?
Man: Let me check the price. Whoa! Um, uh, . . . I guess I'd better not buy it after all.
Woman: Yeah, probably not. Let's go get some food.

Students listening for the main idea, or gist, can easily identify "shopping" as the main topic of conversation, even though the man and woman also discuss getting a bite to eat. They are also able to pick out the specific information, or details; in this case, the item the man wants to buy. To help students understand the idea of inference – listening "between the lines" – ask them whether or not the man has enough money to buy the computer. Even though neither speaker directly says that the man does not have enough money, students can understand that he doesn't. Students come to understand that what they are listening for is just as important as what they are listening to.

Many of these ideas are helpful in understanding the listening process, but they should not be seen as rigid models. We need to remember that listening is actually very complex. A student listening for gist or inference may, for example, get the clues from catching a couple of specific bits of information.

Remember that although listeners need practice in listening, they also need more: They need to learn *how* to listen. They need different types of listening strategies and tasks. They need to learn to preview. Our students need exposure to it all. When students get the exposure they need, they build their listening skills. They become active listeners.

Steven Brown
Dorolyn Smith

Before you begin

How do you learn English?

From the people who wrote this book

Dear Students:

We hope that you learn a lot of English. We also hope that you enjoy learning it.

Do you ever think about how you learn? What things do you do to learn English? What techniques help you learn?

There are many different ways to try to learn. These are called **strategies**. This book will teach you many different strategies. Think about how you learn best. Try to find the strategies that work best for you.

One strategy is **clarification**. When you ask for clarification, you are trying to understand. For example, if you don't understand something, you can say, "Could you repeat that?"

Another strategy is **prediction**. Prediction is when you think about what will happen. You guess what you will hear.

Try the activities in Listening task 1. You will practice predicting and asking for clarification.

Good luck with learning English. You can do it!

Sincerely,
Steven Brown
Dorolyn Smith

What do you say when . . . ?

A Work with a partner. Complete the sentences.

What do you say when . . . ?

1 you want someone to say something again

C_ould___ you r_epeat_____ that?

2 you want to know how to spell a word

H____ d__ _____ spell (that)?

3 you want to know a word in English

H____ d__ ____ say (that) in English?

4 you don't understand something

I don't u_____ .

5 you want to hear the recording again

Once m_____ , p_____ .

6 you understand the meaning but you don't know the answer

__ _____ know.

B Now listen. Were you correct? Write the sentences.

1. *Could you repeat that?*

2. _____

3. _____

4. _____

5. _____

6. _____

What are you listening for?

There are many ways to listen. We listen differently for different reasons.

MAIN IDEA **A** 🎧 **Listen to the conversation. What is the most important idea?**
Check (✓) the correct answer.

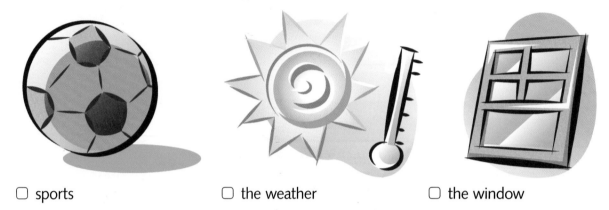

☐ sports ☐ the weather ☐ the window

Sometimes you don't have to understand everything you hear. You just want
the main idea, or general meaning.

DETAILS **B** 🎧 **Listen again. What is the weather like? Check (✓) the correct answer.**

☐ It's sunny. ☐ It's cold. ☐ It's raining.

Sometimes you only need to understand the details, or specific information.
Ask yourself, "What am I listening for?"

INFERENCE **C** 🎧 **Listen again. Is the woman happy? Check (✓) yes or no.**

☐ yes ☐ no

Sometimes people don't say the exact words. You can still understand the meaning.
This is called listening "between the lines," or listening and making inferences.

What are you listening for?

Try it again. Two friends are talking. Each time you listen, think about the information you need.

MAIN IDEA **D** 🎧 Listen. What is the most important idea? Check (✓) the correct answer.

☐ food   ☐ school   ☐ shopping

DETAILS **E** 🎧 Listen again. What does the man want to buy? Circle the correct information.

He wants to buy a *computer* / *cell phone*.

INFERENCE **F** 🎧 Listen again. Does he have enough money? Check (✓) *yes* or *no*.

☐ yes   ☐ no

You heard the same conversation three times. Each time, you listened for different reasons. Always think about why you are listening.

Getting to know you

A What questions are OK to ask when you meet someone for the first time? What questions are not OK to ask? Check (✓) the questions you think are OK to ask.

1. ☑ Are you from around here?
2. ☐ What do you do?
3. ☐ How much money do you make?
4. ☐ Who are you going to vote for?
5. ☐ Where are you from?
6. ☐ Are you married?
7. ☐ How old are you?
8. ☐ Do you like jazz?
9. ☐ Are you going to have children?
10. ☐ It's a beautiful day, isn't it?

B Match each question in Exercise A with a topic below. Write the numbers.

____ age	____ likes and dislikes	____ politics	____ salaries
____ hometowns	____ personal decisions	____ relationships	____ the weather
____ jobs	_1_ where you are right now		

C Work with a partner. Choose three topics you think are OK to ask about. Write one more question for each topic on a separate piece of paper. Then share them with the class.

I wouldn't ask that!

MAIN IDEA **A** 🎧 Listen. People are meeting for the first time. What are they talking about?
Number the topics from 1 to 6. (There are two extra topics.)

____ age	____ likes and dislikes	____ politics	_1_ salaries
____ hometowns	____ where they are right now	____ relationships	____ the weather

INFERENCE **B** 🎧 Listen again. Are the people comfortable with the topics of conversation?
Check (✓) *yes* or *no*.

	yes	no		yes	no
1.	☐	☑	4.	☐	☐
2.	☐	☐	5.	☐	☐
3.	☐	☐	6.	☐	☐

Friends or strangers?

INFERENCE A 🎧 Listen. Are these people talking to friends or strangers? Write *F* (friends) or *S* (strangers).

1 F

2

3

4

DETAILS B 🎧 Listen again. How did you know? Write the words that gave you the hints.

1. *long time, married, remember*

2. _____

3. _____

4. _____

SELF-STUDY *See page 84.*

Nice to meet you.

PREPARE **A** What questions would you like to ask a classmate? Write one more question
for each topic. Then check (✓) five questions to ask.

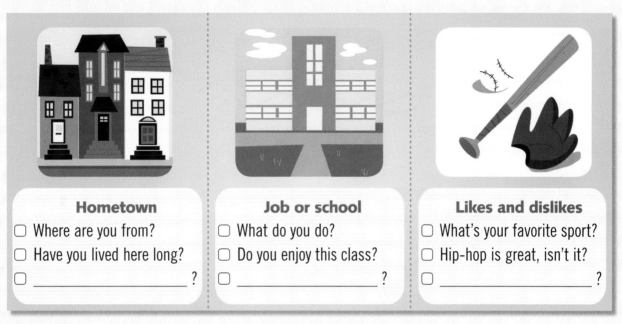

Hometown
- ☐ Where are you from?
- ☐ Have you lived here long?
- ☐ _____ ?

Job or school
- ☐ What do you do?
- ☐ Do you enjoy this class?
- ☐ _____ ?

Likes and dislikes
- ☐ What's your favorite sport?
- ☐ Hip-hop is great, isn't it?
- ☐ _____ ?

PRACTICE **B** **1.** 🎧 Listen and practice. Review the intonation of yes-no questions and
Wh- questions.

Are you a student? ↗   Is this your first trip to Australia? ↗

What kind of music do you like? ↘   Where do you go to school? ↘

2. 🎧 Listen. Do you hear a yes-no question or a *Wh-* question?
Check (✓) the correct answers.

	yes-no	Wh-		yes-no	Wh-		yes-no	Wh-
a.	☑	☐	c.	☐	☐	e.	☐	☐
b.	☐	☐	d.	☐	☐	f.	☐	☐

SPEAK **C** **1. Work with a partner. Take turns asking the questions from Exercise A.**

Hello, my name's Min Hee. I'm from Seoul. Where are you from?

2. Now introduce your partner to the class.

This is Min Hee. She's from Seoul. She's a DJ, and she likes hip-hop.

A Work with a partner. Look at the world map. Which countries would you like to visit?

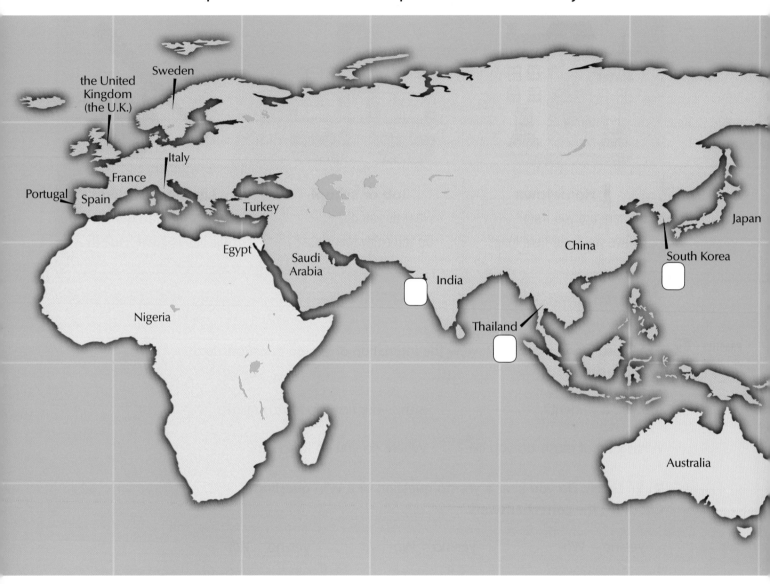

B Work with your partner. What languages do they speak in these countries?
Complete the chart with as many as you can. Then check your answers on page 79.

Country	Languages	Country	Languages	Country	Languages
Australia	*English*	France		South Korea	
Brazil	*Portuguese*	India	*English, Hindi*	Sweden	
Canada		Japan		Thailand	*Thai*
Egypt		Mexico	*Spanish*	Turkey	

Where are you going?

DETAILS **A** 🎧 Listen. People are talking about travel destinations. Where are they going? Number the countries from 1 to 4. (There are two extra countries.)

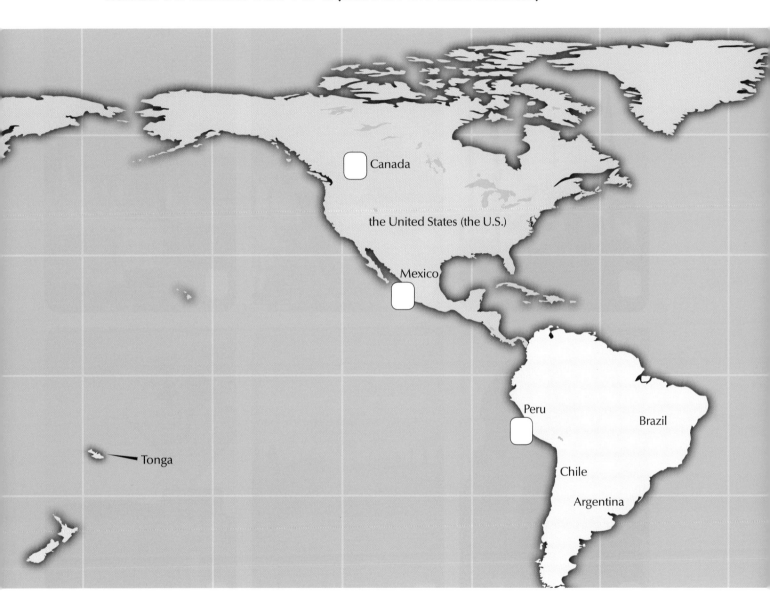

Canada

the United States (the U.S.)

Mexico

Tonga

Peru

Brazil

Chile

Argentina

DETAILS **B** 🎧 Listen again. What are the people going to do there? Check (✓) the correct answers.

1. ☐ work
   ☑ study

2. ☐ live with a family
   ☐ find an apartment

3. ☐ visit a friend
   ☐ start a new job

4. ☐ visit an old friend
   ☐ visit relatives

Where is it?

INFERENCE **A** 🎧 Listen. People are giving information about different countries. Which countries are they talking about? Number the pictures from 1 to 5. (There is one extra picture.)

Turkey

Brazil

1

Canada

Egypt

India

Australia

FOR 15 km

DETAILS **B** 🎧 Listen again. What are the official languages of the countries? Write the languages. (Two of the countries have more than one official language.)

1. *Portuguese*

2. _____

3. _____

4. _____

5. _____

SELF-STUDY *See page 85.*

Let's go!

PREPARE **A** Choose two countries from this unit, or think of other countries you know about.
Then complete the chart.

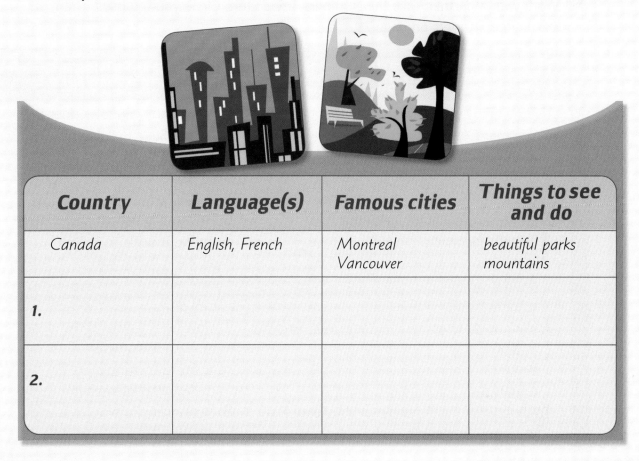

Country	Language(s)	Famous cities	Things to see and do
Canada	English, French	Montreal Vancouver	beautiful parks mountains
1.			
2.			

PRACTICE **B** **1.** 🎧 Listen and practice. Notice the stressed syllables.

English   Spanish   Korean   Chinese

2. 🎧 Circle the stressed syllables. Then listen and check your answers.

a. Arabic   c. Japanese   e. Portuguese

b. Italian   d. Turkish   f. Hindi

SPEAK **C** Work in groups of three. Take turns talking about the countries you chose
in Exercise A. Tell your classmates why they should go there.

> *You should visit Canada. People in Canada speak English
> and French. Montreal has many beautiful parks . . .*

What's the number?

Warming up

A Work with a partner. Take the Numbers Trivia Quiz. Circle your guesses. Then check your answers on page 79.

NUMBERS TRIVIA QUIZ

1. How many sports are there in the Summer Olympic Games?
   a. 28
   b. 47
   c. 52

2. How many countries are in the United Nations?
   a. 175
   b. 191
   c. 201

3. How many languages are there in the world?
   a. 2,501
   b. 4,673
   c. 6,912

4. About how many people climb Mount Fuji in Japan every year?
   a. 125,000
   b. 300,000
   c. 550,000

5. How many windows does the Empire State Building have?
   a. 4,253
   b. 6,500
   c. 7,805

6. How many people have walked on the moon?
   a. 7
   b. 9
   c. 12

7. How far is it around the world?
   a. 40,075 kilometers
   b. 56,782.5 kilometers
   c. 68,649.8 kilometers

8. How many Indonesian islands are there?
   a. 7,670
   b. 17,670
   c. 70,670

B Work with a partner. Cover the right column. Take turns reading the numbers aloud. Then check your answers in the right column.

(413) 555–6154	=	four-one-three, five-five-five, six-one-five-four
6154 East St.	=	Sixty-one fifty-four East Street
8,390	=	eight thousand three hundred ninety
26,455	=	twenty-six thousand four hundred fifty-five
327,000	=	three hundred twenty-seven thousand

The number, please.

MAIN IDEA **A** 🎧 Listen. People are giving information. Number the forms from 1 to 4.

Billing

Name: **Tom**

Credit Card Type: **VISTA**

Credit Card Number:

Expiration Date:

(**Submit**)

☐ online order form

Messages ☎

For _Paula_

Time _11:00 a.m._

From _Jim Robbins_

Phone No. _824-555-2137_

Message _Call him at work._

1 telephone message

Track Your Order

Order Number

Last Name

Postal Code

(**Click Here!**)

☐ shipment tracking form

To: _Mee Sun Park_

Address: _____ _West 145th St._

City/State: _Los Angeles, CA_

Postal Code: _____

☐ mailing label

DETAILS **B** 🎧 Listen again. Complete the forms with the missing information.

Listening task 2
What's the biggest . . . ?

DETAILS **A** 🎧 Listen. People are playing a TV game show about the world's biggest natural wonders. Check (✓) the correct answers.

Mount Kilimanjaro

Mount Everest

1. the tallest mountain ☑ Mount Everest ☐ Mount Kilimanjaro

2. the longest river ☐ the Amazon ☐ the Nile

3. the biggest lake ☐ the Caspian Sea ☐ Lake Superior

4. the tallest waterfall ☐ Angel Falls ☐ Niagara Falls

DETAILS **B** 🎧 Listen again. How big are the natural wonders? Circle the correct answers.

1. (8,850 meters) / 8,050 meters

2. 6,965 kilometers / 6,695 kilometers

3. 438,000 square kilometers / 483,000 square kilometers

4. 970 meters / 979 meters

SELF-STUDY *See page 86.*

Which number?

PREPARE **A** Circle five numbers in the chart. Write how to say the numbers on a separate
piece of paper.

670	70,538	982,012	89,024
52,076	54,999	127,000	17,538
2,017	451,677	617	4,790
982,020	9,333	66,488	233,021
4,719	10,000	528,076	100,000

PRACTICE **B** **1.** 🎧 Listen and practice. Notice that the word *and* may or may not be read.

365   three hundred and sixty-five **or**
       three hundred sixty-five

5,280   five thousand two hundred and eighty **or**
        five thousand two hundred eighty

70,016   seventy thousand and sixteen **or**
         seventy thousand sixteen

188,010   one hundred eighty-eight thousand and ten **or**
          one hundred eighty-eight thousand ten

2. 🎧 Listen. Do you hear *and*? Check (✓) *yes* or *no*.

	yes	no			yes	no			yes	no
a.	☐	☑		c.	☐	☐		e.	☐	☐
b.	☐	☐		d.	☐	☐		f.	☐	☐

SPEAK **C** Work with a partner. Take turns reading your numbers from Exercise A. Circle your
partner's numbers. Then compare your charts. Did you circle all the same numbers?

Body language

A Work with a partner. Look at these examples of body language and gestures. Which ones do you know?

ARRIVING

DEPARTING

MEETING POINT

making eye contact

holding hands

waving

shaking hands

standing close together

hugging

B Complete the chart. Choose three examples of body language and gestures from the picture. What do you think they mean? Write as many meanings as you can.

	Body language and gestures	Meanings
	shaking hands	*hello, good-bye, thank you*
1.		
2.		
3.		

Is it OK?

MAIN IDEA **A** 🎧 Listen. What situations are the people talking about? Number the pictures from 1 to 5. (There is one extra picture.)

DETAILS **B** 🎧 Listen again. How do they feel about the situations? Circle the correct answers.

1. The man feels uncomfortable because
   a. he doesn't know Amy well.
   b. he doesn't like Amy.

2. The woman thinks the man
   a. stands too close.
   b. makes too much eye contact.

3. The woman thinks the people are not
   a. polite.
   b. in love.

4. The woman feels strange because the man
   a. touches her.
   b. stands too close.

5. The husband thinks
   a. his son will feel uncomfortable.
   b. his wife will feel uncomfortable.

Unit 4 Body language **19**

What does it mean?

DETAILS **A** 🎧 Listen. People are comparing gestures from around the world. Which two countries are they talking about? Circle the correct answers.

1 nodding your head

(a.) Brazil
b. France
(c.) Greece

2 raising your eyebrows

a. Peru
b. Spain
c. Tonga

3 tapping your head

a. Argentina
b. Canada
c. Turkey

4 waving your fingers

a. Nigeria
b. South Korea
c. the U.S.

DETAILS **B** 🎧 Listen again. Write the correct information.

Where does the gesture mean . . . ?	country
1. no	*Greece*
2. money	
3. someone is crazy	
4. come here	

20 Unit 4 Body language

SELF-STUDY *See page 87.*

Gestures

PREPARE **A** Think of four people you know. Complete the chart. Write the person and a gesture the person often uses. Then write the meaning of the gesture.

Person	Gesture	Meaning
my mother	*raises her eyebrows*	*She is angry.*
1.		
2.		
3.		
4.		

PRACTICE **B** **1.** 🎧 Listen and practice. Notice the stressed words in these sentences.

It doesn't mean "good-bye"; it means "hello."

My mother raises her eyebrows when she is angry, not hungry.

Tapping your head means "crazy"; it doesn't mean "money."

Standing close together is OK in some places; it isn't OK in others.

2. 🎧 Listen. Check (✓) the two stressed words in each sentence.

a. ☑ is
   ☐ aren't
   ☑ isn't

b. ☐ Spain
   ☐ Turkey
   ☐ Greece

c. ☐ great
   ☐ good
   ☐ bad

d. ☐ elbow
   ☐ head
   ☐ ear

e. ☐ nodding
   ☐ tapping
   ☐ tossing

f. ☐ she
   ☐ they
   ☐ he

SPEAK **C** Work in groups of four. Show the gestures you chose in Exercise A. Student A does the gesture, and the group guesses the meaning. When Student A finishes, change roles.

My sister uses this gesture.

I think it means "Go away!"

No, it doesn't mean "Go away!";
it means "Come here."

Unit 4 Body language   **21**

Listening task 1 • Information

MAIN IDEA **A** 🎧 Listen. People are talking about Morocco. What are the topics? Number the pictures from 1 to 4. (There is one extra picture.)

1

DETAILS **B** 🎧 Listen again. Circle the correct answers.

1. The highest point in northern
   Africa is
   a. 467 meters.
   b. 4,167 meters.

2. Moroccans use their right hands
   a. for eating.
   b. for greeting.

3. Older Moroccans often shake
   hands and then touch
   a. their heads.
   b. their hearts.

4. At night, tourists camp
   a. on the beach.
   b. in a village.

Listening task 2 • Languages

MAIN IDEA **A** 🎧 **Listen. A woman is talking about languages in Morocco. Number the languages from 1 to 5. (There is one extra language.)**

_____ standard Arabic _____ Moroccan Arabic _1_ Berber
_____ English _____ French _____ Spanish

DETAILS **B** 🎧 **Listen again. Which languages from Exercise A does the woman use in each situation? Number the situations from 1 to 5. (There is one extra situation.)**

_____ reading literature   _____ speaking with friends
_____ reading the newspaper   _1_ speaking with relatives
_____ singing traditional songs _____ studying at the university

A What words do you use to describe people? Write at least two more words for each group below.

B Share your words with the class. Then make a list of all the new words for each group in Exercise A on a separate piece of paper.

Who's that?

MAIN IDEA **A** 🎧 **Listen. People are at a party. Who are they talking about? Number the people from 1 to 6. (There are two extra people.)**

DETAILS **B** 🎧 **Listen again. How do the speakers know the people? Circle the correct answers.**

1. a. They're friends.
   b. They work together.

2. a. They're from the same hometown.
   b. They go to the same school.

3. a. He's the man's friend.
   b. He's the man's boss.

4. a. They met in school.
   b. They met in the park.

5. a. He was their teacher.
   b. He was their neighbor.

6. a. He's the man's friend.
   b. He and the man work together.

Different looks

A Listen. A woman is talking about how the actor Johnny Depp looks in different movies. Number the pictures from 1 to 5. (There is one extra picture.)

B Listen again. Do the women agree or disagree about the movies? Check (✓) the correct answers.

	agree	disagree		agree	disagree
1.	✓	☐	4.	☐	☐
2.	☐	☐	5.	☐	☐
3.	☐	☐			

SELF-STUDY *See page 88.*

That's different!

PREPARE **A** Work with a partner. Student A, use this page. Student B, turn to page 78. Don't show your picture to your classmates! Look carefully at what the people look like.

PRACTICE **B** **1.** 🎧 Listen and practice. Notice the intonation of echo questions.

The man has a beard?   Three people?

He's next to the couch?   She has blond hair?

2. 🎧 Listen. Do you hear a question or a statement? Check (✓) the correct answers.

	question	statement		question	statement		question	statement
a.	☐	☑	c.	☐	☐	e.	☐	☐
b.	☐	☐	d.	☐	☐	f.	☐	☐

SPEAK **C** Work with your partner. Talk about the pictures from Exercise A. Use echo questions to check understanding. Circle the differences in your picture. Then compare pictures.

The first man is wearing glasses.

He's wearing glasses? In my picture, the man isn't wearing glasses.

A Complete the Shopping Survey. Circle *a* or *b*, or write your own answer. Then compare your answers with a partner.

Shopping Survey

1. I go shopping
   a. less than three times a month.
   b. more than three times a month.

   other _____ .

2. I prefer to shop
   a. online.
   b. at a store.

   other _____ .

3. I usually buy clothes at
   a. a second-hand store.
   b. a designer shop.

   other _____ .

4. When I need to buy a gift, I go to
   a. the mall.
   b. a discount department store.

   other _____ .

5. I probably spend the most money on
   a. things I really need.
   b. things I want, but don't really need.

   other _____ .

B What other things are in these store departments? Write as many as you can.

Electronics	Health and beauty	Jewelry	Sporting goods
DVD player			

I'll buy it!

INFERENCE **A** 🎧 Listen. People are shopping. Where are they going to buy the things? Check (✓) the correct places.

	the mall	a second-hand store	a designer shop	online
1.	✓	☐	☐	☐
2.	☐	☐	☐	☐
3.	☐	☐	☐	☐
4.	☐	☐	☐	☐

DETAILS **B** 🎧 Listen again. Which ones are they going to buy? Check (✓) the correct pictures.

1

a. ☐   b. ✓

2

a. ☐   b. ☐

3

a. ☐   b. ☐

4

a. ☐   b. ☐

At the store

INFERENCE **A** 🎧 Listen. People are at a department store. Where are they? Number the departments from 1 to 5. (There is one extra department.)

DETAILS **B** 🎧 Listen again. Will the people buy the items? Check (✓) *yes* or *no*.

	yes	no		yes	no
1.	☐	☑	4.	☐	☐
2.	☐	☐	5.	☐	☐
3.	☐	☐			

SELF-STUDY *See page 89.*

Let's shop!

PREPARE **A** Where do you like to go shopping? What do you like to buy? Complete the chart.

Let's Shop!

something expensive you'd like to buy	something you bought that you didn't need to buy	someone you need to buy a gift for
a car	_____	_____
a place you like to buy clothing	something you really need to buy	something you like to buy online
_____	_____	_____
someone you like to shop with	something you like to buy at a second-hand store	a place you like to shop for gifts
_____	_____	_____

PRACTICE **B** **1.** 🎧 Listen and practice. Notice the pronunciation of *to*.

need to = /niːdtə/	like to = /laɪktə/

What's something you need to buy?   Who's someone you like to shop with?
I need to buy a new bag.   I like to shop with my sister.

2. 🎧 Listen. Do you hear *need to* or *like to*? Check (✓) the correct answers.

	need to	like to			need to	like to			need to	like to
a.	✓	☐		c.	☐	☐		e.	☐	☐
b.	☐	☐		d.	☐	☐		f.	☐	☐

SPEAK **C** Work in groups of three. Student A asks Student B a question from Exercise A. Student B answers. Student C asks one more question about the topic. Then change roles.

What's something expensive you'd like to buy?

What kind of car?

I'd like to buy a new car.

Warming up

A Work with a partner. Where do these international dishes come from?
Check your answers on page 79.

Appetizers

Main dishes

Side dishes

shumai
steamed with shrimp
or vegetables

bulgogi
sliced, grilled beef

baked beans
baked with brown sugar

***ceviche**
raw fish in lime juice

tempura
fried seafood
and vegetables

***Niçoise salad**
lettuce, tomatoes, tuna,
boiled green beans

*Pronunciation tips: ceviche = se-VEE-chay /sevi:che/
Niçoise salad = nee-SWAHZ SAH-lahd /ni:swɑz sæled/

B What other foods are served in these ways? Write one food for each way.

baked	boiled	fried	grilled	raw	steamed

C Work with your partner. Take turns talking about your favorite international foods.

I like nan. It's a side dish from India. It's bread baked . . .

Your order, please.

MAIN IDEA **A** 🎧 Listen. People are ordering food in a restaurant. How do they want the dishes prepared? Check (✓) the correct pictures.

1
a. ✓   b. ☐

2
a. ☐   b. ☐

3
a. ☐   b. ☐

4
a. ☐   b. ☐

DETAILS **B** 🎧 Listen again. Do they order an appetizer, a main dish, or a side dish? Check (✓) the correct answers. (Some people order more than one course.)

	appetizer	main dish	side dish
1.	☐	✓	✓
2.	☐	☐	☐
3.	☐	☐	☐
4.	☐	☐	☐

Food and cultures

DETAILS **A** 🎧 Listen. A famous cook is talking about her international cookbook on TV. Match each type of food with two countries. (There is one extra country.)

1 grilled meat

2 rice dishes

3 pasta

4 appetizers

1	Brazil
	China
	France
	India
	Italy
1	Japan
	Mexico
	Spain
	Turkey

DETAILS **B** 🎧 Listen again. How are the foods the same or different? Check (✓) the correct answers.

	same	different
1. the way the food is cooked	✓	☐
2. the spices that are used	☐	☐
3. when the sauce is added	☐	☐
4. when the food is eaten	☐	☐

SELF-STUDY *See page 90.*

Dinner time

PREPARE **A** What would you like for dinner? Look at the menu. Check (✓) your order. Then circle your choices.

Taste of the World Restaurant

Appetizers
- ✓ shumai
  - shrimp / (vegetable)
- ☐ ceviche
  - small / large

Drinks
- ☐ coffee
  - milk / sugar
- ☐ tea
  - hot / iced

Main dishes
- ☐ pasta
  - meat sauce / vegetable sauce
- ☐ curry
  - chicken / beef
- ☐ tempura plate
  - fish / vegetable / mixed

Side dishes
- ☐ potatoes
  - baked / french fries
- ☐ rice
  - steamed / fried
- ☐ Niçoise salad
  - small / medium / large

Desserts
- ☐ fresh fruit plate
  - small / large
- ☐ cake
  - lemon / vanilla

PRACTICE **B** **1.** 🎧 Listen and practice. Notice the intonation of questions of choice.

Is the fish baked or fried?

Would you like vanilla, chocolate, or strawberry ice cream?

Will you bring the salad before the main dish or after the main dish?

Would you like baked potato, potato salad, or french fries?

2. 🎧 Listen. Do you hear two choices or three? Check (✓) the correct answers.

	two	three			two	three			two	three
a.	✓	☐		c.	☐	☐		e.	☐	☐
b.	☐	☐		d.	☐	☐		f.	☐	☐

SPEAK **C** Work with a partner. Student A is a server in a restaurant. Student B is a customer. Take turns ordering from the menu in Exercise A. Then change roles.

I'd like shumai for an appetizer.

Would you like shrimp or vegetable?

Vacations

A Think about your last vacation. Where did you go? What did you do?
Check (✓) the things you did. Then add two more activities.

☐ just rested	☐ took a trip	☐ visited relatives	☐ went to the beach
☐ stayed home	☐ visited a famous place	☐ went hiking	☐ _____
☐ took a tour	☐ visited a museum	☐ went shopping	☐ _____

B Look at the words that describe vacations. Add two words of your own. Are the words
positive or negative? Write *P* (positive) or *N* (negative).

_N_ awful   _P_ exciting   ____ horrible   ____ relaxing   ____ terrific
____ boring   ____ fantastic   ____ interesting   ____ terrible   ____ wonderful
____ _____   ____ _____

C Work with a partner. Describe your last vacation. Use the words and phrases
from Exercises A and B.

I went hiking. It was terrific.

How was your vacation?

MAIN IDEA **A** 🎧 Listen. What did these people do on vacation? Write *W* (Wei), *J* (Julia), *K* (Katie), or *R* (Ryan) in the correct pictures. (There is one extra picture for each pair.)

DETAILS **B** 🎧 Listen again. Check (✓) two words the people use to describe their vacations.

1. **Wei**   **Julia**
   ☑ wonderful   ☐ boring
   ☐ exciting   ☐ relaxing
   ☑ terrific   ☐ interesting

2. **Katie**   **Ryan**
   ☐ exciting   ☐ boring
   ☐ fantastic   ☐ horrible
   ☐ terrific   ☐ relaxing

A trip to forget

MAIN IDEA **A** 🎧 **Listen. Sara and a friend took a vacation to England. What situations is Sara talking about? Number the pictures from 1 to 5. (There is one extra picture.)**

DETAILS **B** 🎧 **Listen again. What were the problems? Circle the correct information.**

1. They left one (day) / week late.

2. They had to find another place to *eat / sleep.*

3. *Buckingham Palace / Trafalgar Square* was closed.

4. They took a *bus / car* there.

5. She thought the clerk said *sixteen / sixty.*

SELF-STUDY *See page 91.*

My vacation

PREPARE **A** Think of a vacation you have taken. Where did you go? What did you do? How would you describe it? Complete the chart with notes about your vacation.

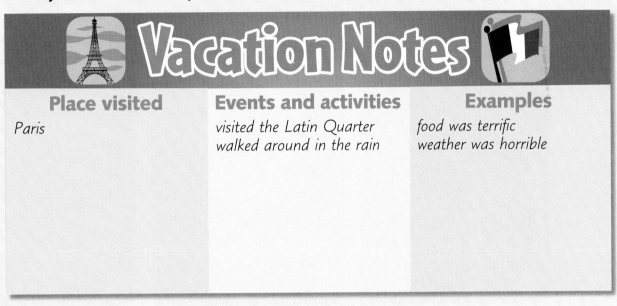

Place visited	Events and activities	Examples
Paris	visited the Latin Quarter walked around in the rain	food was terrific weather was horrible

PRACTICE **B** **1.** Listen and practice. Notice the pronunciation of *-ed* endings.

-ed = /t/	-ed = /d/	-ed = /ɪd/
help → help**ed** talk → talk**ed**	travel → travel**ed** stay → stay**ed**	rest → rest**ed** visit → visit**ed**
_____	_closed_____	_____
_____	_____	_____

2. Write these words in the chart. Then listen and check your answers.

✓closed   happened   liked   needed   rented   shopped

SPEAK **C** Work with a partner. Talk about your vacations from Exercise A.

Last summer, I traveled to Paris.

Really? What did you do there?

I visited the Latin Quarter. The food was terrific!

Listening task 1 • Information

MAIN IDEA **A** 🎧 Listen. People are talking about Malaysia. Which places are they talking about? Number the pictures from 1 to 4. (There is one extra picture.)

Sarawak

Kuala Lumpur

1

Cameron Highlands

Batu Caves

Penang

DETAILS **B** 🎧 Listen again. Circle the correct answers.

1. This place is famous for its
   a. shopping centers.
   b. restaurants.

2. Tourists can see
   a. monkeys.
   b. waterfalls.

3. At night, this place is
   a. quiet.
   b. crowded.

4. In the nearby jungle, there are many
   a. butterflies.
   b. tigers.

Listening task 2 • Night market

A 🎧 **Listen. A man is talking about the Kuala Lumpur night market. What items did he buy? Check (✓) the items. (There are two extra items.)**

B 🎧 **Listen again. There is one mistake in each sentence. Cross out the incorrect words. Then write the correct information.**

1. The market is open at night, but there are lots of ~~lines.~~ *lights*

2. They sell leather jackets at the night market, too.

3. They sell many expensive ones.

4. The man spent fifty minutes bargaining at the night market.

5. The man also recommends fried rice.

6. The man's daughter helped choose the gift.

A Work with a partner. Look at the TV program listings. Which shows would you watch? Which shows wouldn't you watch?

TV Tonight

7:30 P.M.	8:00 P.M.	8:30 P.M.
Newstime with Gordon Santos Weather, sports, local and international news. Special interview tonight with body language expert Carlos Sosa.		**The History of The Beatles** Follow the famous band from their beginnings in Liverpool, England, to worldwide fame.
Morris the Monkey Morris and his friends run away from the zoo and take a fantastic vacation in Hawaii. *1*		**Evening Romance** Will Vicky marry the man from the elevator? Does Jane still love Mike? Find out tonight.
Star Talk Tonight movie star Kylie Jones talks about her new movie and shares her health and beauty secrets.	**Best Friends** This week, watch the comedy as the friends decide to open a restaurant together. Just one problem: Nobody knows how to cook!	
Who Wants to Win $10,000? Two players will answer difficult questions — only one will win!		**Real Wedding** A real couple gets ready for their big day, and our cameras are there.

B Match these types of TV shows with the program listings in Exercise A. Then check your answers on page 79.

1. cartoon	3. game show	5. reality show	7. soap opera
2. documentary	4. the news	6. sitcom	8. talk show

What's on?

INFERENCE **A** 🎧 Listen. A family is deciding what to watch on TV. Who wants to watch the shows? Number the people from 1 to 5. (There is one extra person.)

INFERENCE **B** 🎧 Listen again. What kinds of shows are on? Number the shows from 1 to 5. (There is one extra show.)

____ documentary	____ the news	____ soap opera
____ game show	____ reality show	____ talk show

Reality shows

MAIN IDEA **A** 🎧 Listen to the documentary about reality TV shows. What shows is the narrator talking about? Number the pictures from 1 to 4. (There is one extra picture.)

DETAILS **B** 🎧 Listen again. Are the statements true or false? Check (✓) the correct answers.

	true	false
1. TV viewers choose their favorite singers.	☐	☐
2. The show started in Spain.	☐	☐
3. The U.S. has its own series.	☐	☐
4. The people have to find their own food.	☐	☐

SELF-STUDY *See page 92.*

TV habits

PREPARE **A** Complete the survey about your TV habits. Check (✓) *yes* or *no*.

TV Habits

	yes	no
1. Do you watch TV every day?	☐	☐
2. Are you interested in reality shows?	☐	☐
3. Do you turn off the TV when you aren't watching it?	☐	☐
4. Do you turn on the TV when you first wake up?	☐	☐
5. Are you ever late for school or work because of a TV show?	☐	☐
6. Do you ever watch TV in bed?	☐	☐
7. Do you eat in front of the TV?	☐	☐
8. Are you worried that you watch too much TV?	☐	☐

PRACTICE **B** **1.** Listen and practice. Notice the pronunciation of *Do you* and *Are you* in informal conversation.

Do you = /duyə/	Are you = /aryə/

Do you watch TV every day? Are you interested in reality shows?
Do you watch game shows? Are you going to watch TV tonight?

2. Listen. Do you hear *Do you* or *Are you*? Check (✓) the correct answers.

	Do you	Are you		Do you	Are you		Do you	Are you
a.	✓	☐	c.	☐	☐	e.	☐	☐
b.	☐	☐	d.	☐	☐	f.	☐	☐

SPEAK **C** Work with a partner. Take turns asking and answering the survey questions from Exercise A. Do you think your partner watches too much TV? Why?

Getting there

A Work with a partner. Take turns asking and answering these questions about transportation.

1. How often do you take public transportation?
2. What types of public transportation do you use?
3. Have you used public transportation in a foreign country?

B How did you get to class today? Compare your trip to your partner's.

- Did you have to transfer?
- Whose transportation took longer?
- Whose trip was more expensive?

Visiting Singapore

MAIN IDEA **A** 🎧 **Listen. Some tourists are visiting Singapore. Where do they want to go? Number the places from 1 to 4. (There are two extra places.)**

DETAILS **B** 🎧 **Listen again. How will they get there? Number the types of transportation they will use in order. (There is one extra type for each.)**

1. _1_ subway
   ____ taxi
   _2_ on foot

2. ____ taxi
   ____ cable car
   ____ subway

3. ____ subway
   ____ cable car
   ____ taxi

4. ____ subway
   ____ taxi
   ____ on foot

San Francisco

INFERENCE **A** 🎧 Listen. People are sightseeing in San Francisco. How will they get to their destinations? Check (✓) their choices.

1 Fisherman's Wharf

☐ taxi   ☐ cable car

2 AT&T Park

☐ bus   ☐ subway

3 City Hall

☐ subway   ☐ streetcar

4 Chinatown

☐ cable car   ☐ on foot

5 San Francisco Zoo

☐ streetcar   ☐ bus

DETAILS **B** 🎧 Listen again. Circle the correct information.

1. The taxi ride is *cheaper / more expensive* than the cable car ride.

2. They *have to / don't have to* pay when they transfer.

3. BART costs *more than / the same as* the streetcar.

4. The cable car takes *ten / fifteen* minutes.

5. One child's ticket costs *thirty-five / seventy* cents.

SELF-STUDY *See page 93.*

My town

PREPARE **A** Work with a partner. Think of two interesting places for a visitor to your town or area. Then complete the chart.

Place	Best way to get there	Time	Cost
City Shopping Mall	Take the number 10 bus downtown. Get off at the third stop. Then transfer to the yellow line.	about 20 minutes	$2.00
1.			
2.			

PRACTICE **B** **1.** 🎧 Listen and practice. Notice the pronunciation of ordinal numbers.

Get off at the third traffic light.   The bus stop is on West Fiftieth Street.
Take the Twenty-fifth Street exit.   It's the second building on the left.

2. 🎧 Listen. Check (✓) the numbers you hear.

a. ☐ 3rd   b. ☐ 121st   c. ☐ 16th   d. ☐ 1st   e. ☐ 45th
   ☑ 5th   ☐ 122nd   ☐ 60th   ☐ 3rd   ☐ 54th
   ☐ 6th   ☐ 123rd   ☐ 66th   ☐ 13th   ☐ 64th

SPEAK **C** Join another pair. Give directions to the places you chose in Exercise A. Can the other pair guess the place?

Take the number 10 bus downtown. Get off at the third stop. Then transfer to the yellow line. It takes . . .

Is it the art museum?

World market

Warming up

A Work in groups of three. Take the Export Quiz. Guess which country sells the most of each product. Write your group's guess under each product.

I think Australia sells the most beef.

EXPORT QUIZ

☑ Australia ☐ China ☐ Saudi Arabia
☐ Brazil ☐ India ☐ Thailand
☐ Canada ☐ Japan ☐ the U.S.

rice

beef

Australia

wheat

leather shoes

tea

automobiles

coffee

oil

wood products

B Check your group's answers on page 79. Which group had the most correct answers?

International marketplace

INFERENCE **A** Listen. People are shopping at an international market. Which markets will they visit? Number the markets from 1 to 5. (There is one extra market.)

International Market

Thailand

France

Australia

Canada

Turkey

Mexico

DETAILS **B** Listen again. What do they want to buy? Write the correct information.

1. _a leather bag_

2. _____

3. _____

4. _____

5. _____

It's good business.

DETAILS **A** 🎧 Listen. Companies changed their products to sell them in different parts of the world. Write the places the products were changed for. Then check (✓) the correct changes.

1 Campbell's®

2 A vacation company

Place _United Kingdom_

Change ☐ took out the water
☐ added water

Place _____

Change ☐ offered shorter stays
☐ offered longer stays

3 McDonald's®

4 Häagen-Dazs®

Place _____

Change ☐ made burgers without beef
☐ made burgers with less beef

Place _____

Change ☐ changed the colors
☐ changed the flavors

DETAILS **B** 🎧 Listen again. Why did the companies change the products? Circle the correct information.

1. People thought the product was *easy* / *difficult* to prepare.

2. This company is popular with *Australians* / *Europeans*.

3. People didn't buy the product because of their *religion* / *health*.

4. This company wanted *adults* / *children* to enjoy their product.

SELF-STUDY *See page 94.*

International fair

PREPARE **A** Think of a country you know well. What kinds of products is it known for?
Complete the chart.

	(country name)		
Food or drink	**Handmade goods**	**Clothing**	**Other**
coffee	wood furniture	leather coats	diamonds

PRACTICE **B** **1.** 🎧 Listen and practice. Notice the contractions for *there is* and *there are*.*

There's a nice video camera.   I heard there's a really fast computer.
There're some beautiful wood products.   Do you know if there're any leather goods?

*These contractions are most common in spoken English.

2. 🎧 Listen. Do you hear the contraction for *there is* or *there are?* Check (✓)
the correct answers.

	there is	there are		there is	there are		there is	there are
a.	☐	✓	c.	☐	☐	e.	☐	☐
b.	☐	☐	d.	☐	☐	f.	☐	☐

SPEAK **C** **1.** Work in groups of three. You are organizing an international fair. Compare your
lists of products from Exercise A. Then choose five products to display.

2. Tell the class what products you chose to display. How many different products
did the class choose?

> *There're many different kinds of handmade
> goods. There's wood furniture. There're . . .*

A Work with a partner. What can people do to save the earth's environment? Label the pictures with phrases from the box. Then add some ideas of your own.

- ☐ bring a cloth bag to the supermarket
- ☐ recycle the newspaper
- ☐ turn off extra lights
- ☑ carpool to work
- ☐ take shorter showers

What can people do...?

to save gasoline
carpool to work
_____
_____

to save trees
_____
_____
_____

to save electricity
_____
_____
_____
_____

to save water
_____
_____
_____

to make less garbage
_____
_____
_____

B Share your ideas from Exercise A with the class. How many different ideas does the class have for saving the environment?

To save gasoline, people can carpool to work.

Helping the environment

INFERENCE **A** 🎧 Listen. Eric is talking to people about the environment. Where are they? Number the pictures from 1 to 5. (There is one extra picture.)

DETAILS **B** 🎧 Listen again. What does Eric recommend to help the environment? Circle the correct answers.

1. a. stop buying the newspaper
   b. recycle the newspaper

2. a. bring a cup
   b. buy a cup

3. a. use a cloth bag
   b. use a paper bag

4. a. take cold showers
   b. take shorter showers

5. a. take the bus
   b. carpool together

Recycling

A 🎧 Listen. All of these materials can be recycled in the U.S. Check (✓) the ones the speaker mentions. (There are two extra items.)

B 🎧 Listen again. How much of these materials do people in the U.S. use or throw away each year? Number the sentences from 1 to 5.

People use enough . . . .

_____ to build a wall from Los Angeles to New York

_____ to fill a soccer stadium 45 times

_____ to fill the two tallest buildings in Chicago every two weeks

_____ to fill the Empire State Building 20 times

_____ to circle the earth four times

SELF-STUDY *See page 95.*

Helping out

PREPARE **A** Work in groups of three. How can you make a difference? Think of a project your class can do to help the environment. Complete the chart.

Project Ideas

Project	How it'll help the environment	How we'll do it
recycling fair	People won't waste so much paper. It'll save trees.	Students will bring old newspapers to school to recycle.

PRACTICE **B** **1.** 🎧 Listen and practice. Notice the contractions for *will* and *will not*.

Our class'll have a recycling fair.   We'll all use public transportation.
We won't waste electricity.   The students won't throw paper away.

2. 🎧 Listen. Do you hear the contraction for *will* or *will not*? Check (✓) the correct answers.

	will	will not		will	will not		will	will not
a.	☐	✓	c.	☐	☐	e.	☐	☐
b.	☐	☐	d.	☐	☐	f.	☐	☐

SPEAK **C** Take turns telling the class about your project from Exercise A. How many different ideas did the class think of?

> We'll have a recycling fair. People won't waste so much paper. It'll save . . .

Listening task 1 • Information

MAIN IDEA **A**  Listen. People are talking about Hungary. What are the topics? Circle the correct answers.

1. a. the environment
   b. exports

2. a. the capital city
   b. the countryside

3. a. food
   b. music

4. a. education
   b. transportation

DETAILS **B** Listen again. Are the statements true or false? Check (✓) the correct answers.

	true	false
1. The land is good for farming.	☐	☐
2. It is famous for its public baths.	☐	☐
3. Paprika is a traditional Hungarian dance.	☐	☐
4. Hungary has five neighboring countries.	☐	☐

Listening task 2 • Souvenirs

A 🎧 **Listen. A woman is talking about handmade goods and souvenirs from Hungary. Number the pictures from 1 to 4. (There is one extra picture.)**

B 🎧 **Listen again. Circle the correct answers.**

1. Hungarians wear this when they
   a. date.
   b. dance.

2. Tourists often buy these to
   a. decorate their houses.
   b. give as wedding gifts.

3. A traditional Hungarian dish is
   a. stuffed pasta.
   b. stuffed peppers.

4. The woman learned this from her
   a. grandmother.
   b. mother.

Warming up

A Read the magazine article about stress and health. Which relaxation techniques would you try? Which ones wouldn't you try?

STRESSED OUT?
Relax. It's good for your health!

Try meditation
Feel calmer and sleep better at night. Meditating just a few minutes every day can help your health.

Try aromatherapy
Aromatherapists say that some smells can give you more energy, and others can help you feel calmer.

Get a massage
Feel younger and have more energy. Massage therapy helps relax the body, and that helps relax the mind.

Drink herbal tea
Feel calmer and sleep better. Have a cup of tea instead of coffee!

Join a yoga class
People who do yoga regularly say they have more energy and look younger!

B What kinds of situations make you feel stressed out? What techniques do you use to relieve stress? Tell the class.

> *I feel stressed out the night before I have to take a test. I usually take a hot bath and try to relax.*

Relax!

A 🎧 Listen. Mia is feeling stressed out. What activities does her friend suggest? Number the activities from 1 to 5. (There is one extra activity.)

B 🎧 Listen again. Will Mia follow her friend's suggestions? Check (✓) *yes* or *no*.

	yes	no			yes	no
1.	☐	☐		4.	☐	☐
2.	☐	☐		5.	☐	☐
3.	☐	☐				

What's it good for?

INFERENCE **A**  Listen. People are talking about health and relaxation. Where are they? Circle the correct answers.

1. a. a tea shop
   b. a sports gym

2. a. a doctor's office
   b. an aromatherapist's office

3. a. a yoga class
   b. a massage therapist's office

4. a. a sports gym
   b. a health food store

5. a. a doctor's office
   b. a yoga class

DETAILS **B**  Listen again. Check (✓) the two health benefits for each technique.

	sleep better	feel younger	look younger	have more energy	feel calmer
1.					
2.					
3.					
4.					
5.					

SELF-STUDY *See page 96.*

Feeling healthy

A Think of two health habits you would like to change. What are some techniques you can use to change the habits? Complete the chart.

Health habit	Technique
sleep better	drink herbal tea before bed
	don't exercise in the evening
1.	
2.	

B **1.** 🎧 **Listen and practice. Notice the pronunciation of *Don't you* and *Why don't you*.**

Don't you = /dontʃə/	Why don't you = /wai dontʃə/

Don't you enjoy exercising?   Why don't you try getting a massage?
Don't you feel calmer after drinking herbal tea?   Why don't you get some exercise?

2. 🎧 **Listen. Do you hear *Don't you* or *Why don't you*? Check (✓) the correct answers.**

	Don't you	Why don't you		Don't you	Why don't you		Don't you	Why don't you
a.	☐	☑	c.	☐	☐	e.	☐	☐
b.	☐	☐	d.	☐	☐	f.	☐	☐

C Work with a partner. Take turns talking about the health habits you would like to change from Exercise A. Can you suggest more techniques to help your partner?

> *I'd like to sleep better. I could drink herbal tea before bed.*

> *Yeah, and I have another idea. Why don't you try jogging during the day?*

Personalities

A What kind of person are you? Take the Personality Survey. Check (✓) *T* (true) or *F* (false).

Personality Survey What kind of person are you?

	T	F	Personality trait
1. People say I have a lot of energy. I'm always active.	✓	☐	*energetic*
2. I enjoy meeting new people at parties.	☐	☐	
3. I like to draw, paint, play music, or dance.	☐	☐	
4. I often lose things or don't remember information.	☐	☐	
5. I get angry or upset with people easily.	☐	☐	
6. I dream about being rich or famous.	☐	☐	
7. I think it's important to win at sports or games.	☐	☐	
8. I love to travel and have new experiences.	☐	☐	
9. My friends can always rely on me.	☐	☐	
10. I'm usually relaxed. I don't get stressed out easily.	☐	☐	

B Work with a partner. What personality traits do the statements in Exercise A describe? Match the words from the box with the statements.

☐ adventurous	☐ competitive	☐ dependable	✓ energetic	☐ short-tempered
☐ ambitious	☐ creative	☐ easygoing	☐ forgetful	☐ sociable

C Choose three words from the box that describe your personality. Tell your partner.

I think I'm ambitious, creative, and dependable.

People are different.

INFERENCE **A** Listen. People are talking. Where are they? Number the pictures from 1 to 5. (There is one extra picture.)

INFERENCE **B** Listen again. Which word best describes the first speaker? Circle the correct answers.

1. a. forgetful
   b. competitive

2. a. adventurous
   b. energetic

3. a. sociable
   b. creative

4. a. adventurous
   b. dependable

5. a. ambitious
   b. short-tempered

Two of a kind

MAIN IDEA **A** 🎧 **Listen. People are describing the personalities of people they know. What are the people's relationships? Circle the correct answers.**

1. a. sisters
   b. mother and daughter

2. a. co-workers
   b. roommates

3. a. husband and wife
   b. neighbors

4. a. college friends
   b. father and son

5. a. brothers
   b. classmates

INFERENCE **B** 🎧 **Listen again. Are their personalities similar or different? Check (✓) the correct answers.**

	similar	different		similar	different
1.	☐	☐	4.	☐	☐
2.	☐	☐	5.	☐	☐
3.	☐	☐			

SELF-STUDY *See page 97.*

A person I know

PREPARE **A** Think of two friends or family members. Complete the chart. Write two personality traits that describe the people. Then write an example for each trait.

Person	Personality trait	Examples
My sister Claire	forgetful	forgot her own birthday
	energetic	goes jogging at 6:00 A.M.

PRACTICE **B** **1.** 🎧 Listen and practice. Notice the stress for emphasis.

My brother is so creative.   They are very competitive.
She's really short-tempered.   Our personalities are so different.

2. 🎧 Listen. Do you hear *so, really,* or *very*? Check (✓) the correct answers.

	so	really	very			so	really	very			so	really	very
a.	☐	☐	☑		c.	☐	☐	☐		e.	☐	☐	☐
b.	☐	☐	☐		d.	☐	☐	☐		f.	☐	☐	☐

SPEAK **C** Work with a partner. Take turns sharing information about the people you chose in Exercise A. Is your personality similar to or different from the people's?

My sister Claire is very forgetful . . .

Youth culture

A Complete the Ideal Age Survey. Write your answers to the questions.

Ideal Age Survey

At what age is it OK for people to . . . ?

	Me	My partner
live on their own		
get a full-time job		
travel abroad alone		
go on a date		
get a driver's license		
get married		
have a credit card		
have a baby		

B Work with a partner. Take turns asking the questions in Excercise A. Write your partner's answers. Do you and your partner agree on all the ages?

At what age is it OK for people to live on their own?

I think it's OK at 21.

Decisions

MAIN IDEA **A** 🎧 Listen. What decisions are the people trying to make? Number the decisions from 1 to 5. (There is one extra decision.)

_____ buying a car   _____ getting a job   _____ living alone

_____ buying a house   _____ getting married   _____ traveling abroad

INFERENCE **B** 🎧 Listen again. Will the people decide to do the things? Check (✓) _yes_ or _no_.

	yes	no		yes	no
1.	☐	☐	4.	☐	☐
2.	☐	☐	5.	☐	☐
3.	☐	☐			

Coming of age

MAIN IDEA **A** 🎧 **Listen. People are talking about coming-of-age ceremonies. What countries are they talking about? Number the pictures from 1 to 5. (There is one extra picture.)**

Norway

the U.S.

Ghana

Mexico

Kenya

Japan

DETAILS **B** 🎧 **Listen again. When do the ceremonies happen? Circle the correct answers.**

1. a. at age 20
   b. at age 21

2. a. at age 15
   b. at age 16

3. a. after marriage
   b. before marriage

4. a. at high school graduation
   b. at college graduation

5. a. the first year of high school
   b. the last year of high school

SELF-STUDY *See page 98.*

Changes

PREPARE **A** How has your life changed since you were younger? Complete the chart. Write two things you used to do and two things you didn't use to do.

When I was younger, . . .

I used to be a server.	I didn't use to have a full-time job.
1.	1.
2.	2.

PRACTICE **B** **1.** Listen and practice. Notice the pronunciation of *used to* and *didn't use to*.

used to = /yuwstə/	didn't use to = /dɪdnt yuwstə/

My parents used to give me money.
I used to take the train to school.

I didn't use to make so many decisions.
I didn't use to have my own car.

2. Listen. Do you hear *used to* or *didn't use to*? Check (✓) the correct answers.

	used to	didn't use to		used to	didn't use to		used to	didn't use to
a.	✓	☐	c.	☐	☐	e.	☐	☐
b.	☐	☐	d.	☐	☐	f.	☐	☐

SPEAK **C** Work with a partner. Take turns talking about the things you used to and didn't use to do from Exercise A. Did you and your partner use to do any of the same things?

I used to be a server in a restaurant.

Me, too! I used to work at a coffee shop.

I didn't use to have a full-time job.

A Look at these common themes and symbols in dreams. Check (✓) the things you have dreamed about.

☐ animals	☐ flying	☐ spiders or spiderwebs
☐ being chased	☐ a haunted house	☐ taking a test
☐ falling	☐ money	☐ teeth

B Work with a partner. Compare your answers from Exercise A. How many of the same things have you dreamed about? Were the dreams good dreams or nightmares?

The meaning of dreams

MAIN IDEA **A** 🎧 Listen. People are describing their dreams to a dream interpreter. What happens in each dream? Number the pictures in the correct order from 1 to 3.

DETAILS **B** 🎧 Now listen to the dream interpreter. What does he say is the real meaning of the dreams? Check (✓) the correct answers.

1. She doesn't like something about
   - ☐ her bedroom.
   - ☑ herself.

2. He's worried about
   - ☐ changing his life.
   - ☐ losing his pen.

3. She will
   - ☐ get over her problem.
   - ☐ never have problems.

4. She's excited about
   - ☐ taking a trip.
   - ☐ making money.

The dream catcher

DETAILS **A** 🎧 **Listen. A man is explaining Native American dream catchers. Circle the correct information.**

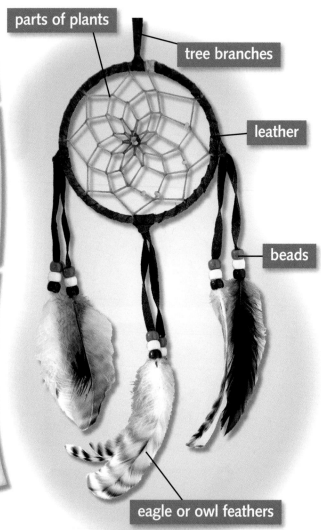

parts of plants

tree branches

leather

beads

eagle or owl feathers

> **D**ream catchers are a tradition of the Chippewa Indian tribe from the U.S. and *Canada / Mexico*. Grandparents usually make dream catchers as gifts for new *neighbors / babies*. The dream catchers are made from trees and plants, and are decorated with beads, *paper / leather*, and feathers. Owl feathers are for girls, and eagle feathers are for boys. Chippewa families put the dream catchers *above / under* their babies' beds at night. They believe that good dreams will go through the center of the dream catcher, and *spiders / nightmares* will get caught in the web and will not reach the baby.

MAIN IDEA **B** 🎧 **Now listen to the dream catcher legend. Number the sentences in the correct order from 1 to 8.**

____ One day, her grandson came in and saw the spider.

_8_ The spider said, "Now you will have only good dreams."

____ The grandmother asked her grandson not to kill the spider.

_1_ A grandmother was watching a spider making a web.

____ The spider said, "I will give you a gift."

____ The spider thanked the grandmother for saving his life.

____ He picked up a shoe to hit the spider.

____ The spider had made a beautiful web near the window.

SELF-STUDY *See page 99.*

In my dreams

PREPARE **A** Think of a dream you have had. Complete the chart. Write the place where the dream happened. Then write the people, symbols, and events you saw in the dream.

Place	People and symbols	Events
at my office	my co-worker, my boss, a tiger	chased by a tiger

PRACTICE **B** **1.** 🎧 Listen and practice. Notice the rhythm of complex sentences.

In the dream I had last night, my co-worker was a tiger.

When I arrived at the office, he started to chase me.

After I got away, he started to chase my boss.

When I woke up, I was very confused.

2. 🎧 Listen again. Do you hear a complex sentence? Check (✓) *yes* or *no*.

	yes	no		yes	no		yes	no
a.	☐	✓	c.	☐	☐	e.	☐	☐
b.	☐	☐	d.	☐	☐	f.	☐	☐

SPEAK **C** Work in groups of three. Take turns telling your dreams from Exercise A. Can you guess the meaning of your classmates' dreams?

> In the dream I had last night, my co-worker . . .

Listening task 1 • Information

MAIN IDEA **A** 🎧 **Listen. People are talking about Hawaii. What are the topics? Circle the correct answers.**

1. a. clothing styles
   b. hairstyles

2. a. work
   b. relaxation

3. a. transportation
   b. vacation

4. a. music
   b. dance

DETAILS **B** 🎧 **Listen again. Circle the correct information.**

1. Many businesses have Aloha *Mondays / Fridays*.

2. Hawaii has a lot of *spas / hotels*.

3. *Tourists / Traffic* can be a problem in Honolulu.

4. The hula is a traditional *song / dance*.

Listening task 2 • Graduation day

MAIN IDEA **A** 🎧 **Listen. A man is talking about high school graduation events in Hawaii. Number the pictures from 1 to 5. (There is one extra picture.)**

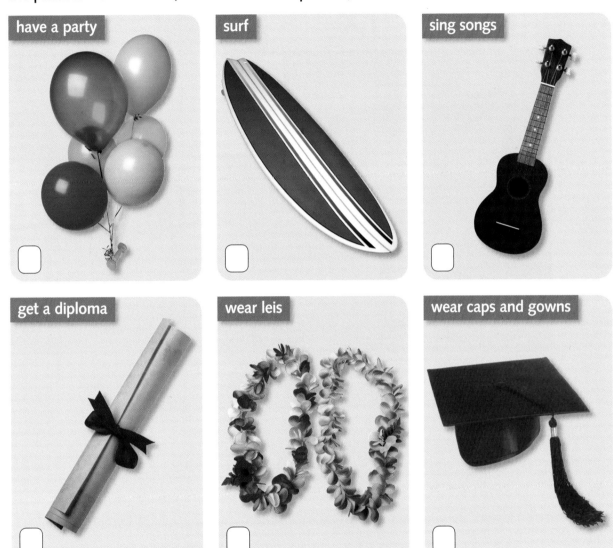

have a party

surf

sing songs

get a diploma

wear leis

wear caps and gowns

DETAILS **B** 🎧 **Listen again. Circle the correct information.**

1. Girls and boys wear *the same thing / something different.*

2. *Teachers / Students* write one every year.

3. Students receive these from *their parents / the principal.*

4. This tradition is *old / new.*

5. This happens at *school / a restaurant.*

Appendix   Unit 5 · *That's different!*

PREPARE **A** Work with a partner. Student B, use this page. Don't show your picture to your classmates! Look carefully at what the people look like.

PRACTICE **B** **1.** 🎧 Listen and practice. Notice the intonation of echo questions.

The man has a beard?   Three people?

He's next to the couch?   She has blond hair?

2. 🎧 Listen. Do you hear a question or a statement? Check (✓) the correct answers.

	question	statement		question	statement		question	statement
a.	☐	✓	c.	☐	☐	e.	☐	☐
b.	☐	☐	d.	☐	☐	f.	☐	☐

SPEAK **C** Work with your partner. Talk about the pictures from Exercise A. Use echo questions to check understanding. Circle the differences in your picture. Then compare pictures.

> *The first man is wearing glasses.*

> *He's wearing glasses? In my picture, the man isn't wearing glasses.*

Answer key

Unit 2 Going places
Page 10
Warming up Exercise A

Country	Languages	Country	Languages	Country	Languages
Australia	English	France	French	South Korea	Korean
Brazil	Portuguese	India	English, Hindi	Sweden	Swedish
Canada	English, French	Japan	Japanese	Thailand	Thai
Egypt	Arabic	Mexico	Spanish	Turkey	Turkish

Unit 3 What's the number?
Page 14
Warming up Exercise A

1. a. 28
2. b. 191
3. c. 6,912
4. b. 300,000
5. b. 6,500
6. c. 12
7. a. 40,075 km
8. b. 17,670

Unit 7 International food
Page 32
Warming up Exercise A

shumai China
ceviche Peru / Ecuador
bulgogi Korea
tempura Japan
baked beans the U.S.
Niçoise salad France

Unit 9 TV
Page 42
Warming up Exercise A

1. **cartoon** *Morris the Monkey*
2. **documentary** *The History of The Beatles*
3. **game show** *Who Wants to Win $10,000?*
4. **the news** *Newstime with Gordon Santos*
5. **reality show** *Real Wedding*
6. **sitcom** *Best Friends*
7. **soap opera** *Evening Romance*
8. **talk show** *Star Talk*

Unit 11 World market
Page 50
Warming up Exercise B

rice Thailand
leather shoes China
coffee Brazil
beef Australia
tea India
oil Saudi Arabia
wheat the U.S.
automobiles Japan
wood products Canada

Activation

A speaking and listening game

- Work in groups of four.
- Put a marker on "Start."
- Close your eyes. Touch the "How many spaces?" box with a pencil. Move that many spaces.
- Follow the instructions.
- Take turns.

Show a gesture or expression that means
* Come here!
* That's crazy!
* I don't know.

Talk about a person you met recently. Who was he or she? How did you meet?

What's something you do to help the environment?

Start

Finish

Name two products your country exports.

What are two ways you like to relax?

Say three words that describe your personality.

Tell about something that happened when you were traveling.

Name three things that are different about your appearance now and ten years ago.

Explain how people in your country greet
* for the first time.
* old friends.

What is a situation that makes you feel stressed out? What is a situation that makes you feel relaxed?

How many people's phone numbers can you say from memory in one minute? Whose numbers are they?

Talk about a dream you had recently. What do you think it means?

At what age do you think someone is an adult?

YOU CAN ASK ANY PLAYER ONE QUESTION.

Where do you like to shop? What do you usually buy there?

What personality words describe your best friend?

What are three of your favorite international foods?

What is your favorite TV show? Why?

What kinds of transportation are there in your city? Which ones do you use?

Who are some of your favorite TV actors?

Do you want to change anything about the way you look? What is it?

Think of a number between 100 and 10,000. Write it down. Each player has two chances to guess the number. Whose guess is the closest?

YOU CAN ASK ANY PLAYER ONE QUESTION.

Talk about an interesting vacation that you took.

What are some decisions young people have to make when they become adults?

Tell about a vacation you would like to take.

How many hours of TV do you watch each week? What kinds of shows do you watch?

Tell about something you didn't need to buy but you bought anyway.

What country would you like to visit? Why?

How many things do you have with you that are from other countries?

In how many languages can you say "hello"? How about "thank you"?

How many spaces?					
2	1	3	1	3	2
1	3	4	2	3	1
3	1	2	1	2	3
1	2	1	3	5	2
3	5	2	1	2	3
2	1	3	4	3	1

What is the most useful invention in the world?

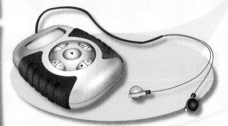

Give directions to your favorite restaurant.

What are three foods that are most typical in your country?

ANY PLAYER CAN ASK YOU ONE QUESTION.

How many gestures can you think of in one minute? Say what they mean.

Listening tips

Here are some listening tips to help you become an active listener.

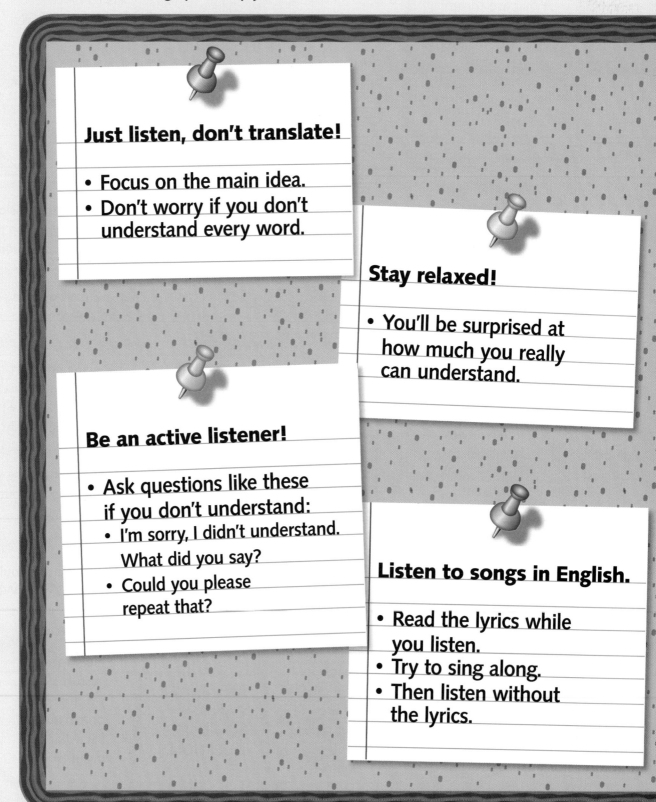

Just listen, don't translate!

- Focus on the main idea.
- Don't worry if you don't understand every word.

Stay relaxed!

- You'll be surprised at how much you really can understand.

Be an active listener!

- Ask questions like these if you don't understand:
  - I'm sorry, I didn't understand. What did you say?
  - Could you please repeat that?

Listen to songs in English.

- Read the lyrics while you listen.
- Try to sing along.
- Then listen without the lyrics.

Watch movies in English.

- Watch a small part of the movie at a time.
- Replay scenes as many times as you'd like.

Use the phone to practice English.

- Speak with friends from your class or other English-speaking friends.
- Agree to speak only English for a specific time.

Call places with answering machines in English.

- Have a listening goal. Listen for a specific piece of information.

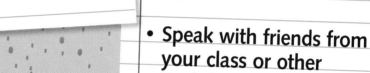

Listen to radio or news programs in English.

- Choose stories to listen to that you know something about.

Self-study

Unit 1

A **1.** 🎧 **Listen to the conversation.**

2. 🎧 **Listen again. Circle the correct answers.**

1. Morgan and Josh are
   a. friends.
   b. strangers.
   c. husband and wife.

2. The party is at
   a. Josh's house.
   b. Morgan's house.
   c. a restaurant.

3. Morgan likes
   a. dancing.
   b. jazz music.
   c. eating.

4. Morgan asks Josh about his
   a. relationship.
   b. religion.
   c. salary.

5. Morgan's question makes Josh
   a. happy.
   b. uncomfortable.
   c. comfortable.

B 🎧 **Listen. Write your answers. You need to know these shapes.**
circle = ●   diamond = ◆   square = ■   star = ★   triangle = ▲

Unit 2

A **1.** 🎧 **Listen to the conversation.**

2. 🎧 **Listen again. Circle the correct answers.**

1. Ashley is going to Thailand
   a. to work.
   b. to study.
   c. for vacation.

2. She is probably going to speak
   a. only English.
   b. English and Thai.
   c. only Thai.

3. She is going to study the language
   a. at a language school.
   b. at the library.
   c. at a university.

4. She is going for
   a. one month.
   b. one week.
   c. two weeks.

5. She is going to visit
   a. one country.
   b. two countries.
   c. more than two countries.

B 🎧 **Listen. Check (✓) *yes* or *no*. Then write your answers.**

	yes	no	
1.	☐	☐	_____
2.	☐	☐	_____
3.	☐	☐	_____
4.	☐	☐	_____
5.	☐	☐	_____

Unit 3

A **1.** 🎧 Listen to the information.

2. 🎧 Listen again. Circle the correct answers.

1. The flight number is
   a. 2072.
   b. 7212.
   c. 1272.

2. The plane is going to
   a. Seattle.
   b. New York.
   c. Los Angeles.

3. Now the plane is flying at
   a. 70,250 meters.
   b. 7,025 meters.
   c. 7,250 meters.

4. The current speed is
   a. 750 kilometers per hour.
   b. 7,050 kilometers per hour.
   c. 7,500 kilometers per hour.

5. People can get up when the plane reaches
   a. 10,006 meters.
   b. 10,060 meters.
   c. 10,600 meters.

B 🎧 Listen. Follow the instructions.

1. _____

2. _____

3. _____

4. _____

5. _____

Unit 4

A **1.** 🎧 **Listen to the conversation.**

2. 🎧 **Listen again. Circle the correct answers.**

1. The people are talking about
   a. a friend.
   b. their professor.
   c. someone they don't know.

2. The man is Ramon's
   a. roommate.
   b. classmate.
   c. brother.

3. The woman thinks Ramon
   a. stands too close.
   b. makes too much eye contact.
   c. hugs her too much.

4. The man thinks Ramon doesn't
   a. know about the problem.
   b. like the woman.
   c. enjoy living in the U.S.

5. The people will probably
   a. stop talking to Ramon.
   b. not look at Ramon.
   c. tell Ramon the problem.

B 🎧 **Listen. Check (✓) yes or no. Then write your answers.**

	yes	no	
1.	☐	☐	_____
2.	☐	☐	_____
3.	☐	☐	_____
4.	☐	☐	_____
5.	☐	☐	_____

Unit 5

A **1.** 🎧 **Listen to the conversation.**

2. 🎧 **Listen again. Circle the correct answers.**

1. The women are at
   a. a party.
   b. school.
   c. an airport.

2. The woman has
   a. long, dark hair.
   b. short, blond hair.
   c. dark, curly hair.

3. Jin is the woman's
   a. sister.
   b. neighbor.
   c. friend.

4. Jin's brother
   a. teaches English.
   b. studies Korean.
   c. teaches Korean.

5. Jin's brother has
   a. glasses.
   b. long, dark hair.
   c. short, dark hair.

B 🎧 **Listen. Follow the instructions.**

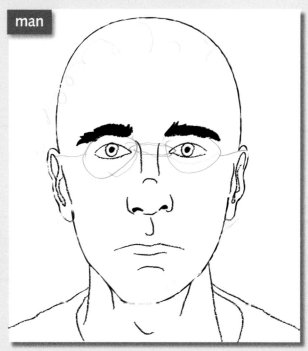

man

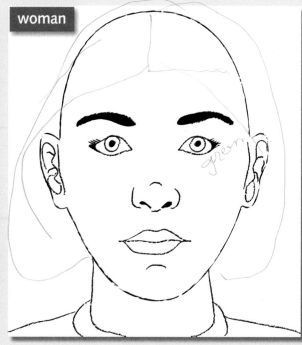

woman

Unit 6

A **1.** 🎧 Listen to the conversation.

2. 🎧 Listen again. Circle the correct answers.

1. The man is shopping
   a. in a mall.
   b. at a small store.
   c. online.

2. The man wants to buy
   a. a jacket.
   b. a suit.
   c. winter gloves.

3. The woman likes
   a. the red one.
   b. the blue one.
   c. the green one.

4. The man decides to buy
   a. a blue one.
   b. a red one.
   c. a green one.

5. The final price is
   a. less than at the mall.
   b. the same as at the mall.
   c. more than at the mall.

B 🎧 Listen. Check (✓) *yes* or *no*. Then write your answers.

	yes	no	
1.	☐	☐	_____
2.	☐	☐	_____
3.	☐	☐	_____
4.	☐	☐	_____
5.	☐	☐	_____

Unit 7

A 1. 🎧 **Listen to the conversation.**

2. 🎧 **Listen again. Circle the correct answers.**

1. The people are at
   a. the man's home.
   b. a restaurant.
   c. the woman's home.

2. The woman likes to eat
   a. everything.
   b. spicy things.
   c. sweet things.

3. The woman is going to have
   a. an appetizer.
   b. an appetizer and a main dish.
   c. a side dish and a dessert.

4. The man is going to have
   a. sushi.
   b. a salad.
   c. tempura.

5. The man is also going to order
   a. a dessert.
   b. a salad.
   c. a drink.

B 🎧 **Listen. Different servers are taking your order. Write the item. Then check (✓) your order.**

1. _sandwich_
   ☐ sliced chicken   ☐ fish   ☐ grilled steak

2. _pasta_
   ☐ appetizer   ☐ main dish   ☐ side dish

3. _fish_
   ☐ baked   ☐ grilled   ☐ fried

4. _shrimp_
   ☐ shrimp   ☐ beef   ☐ vegetable

5. _potatoes_
   ☐ baked   ☐ fried   ☐ salad

Unit 8

A **1.** 🎧 **Listen to the conversation.**

2. 🎧 **Listen again. Circle the correct answers.**

1. The woman thought her vacation was
   a. awful.
   b. wonderful.
   c. exciting.

2. The woman thought the famous places were
   a. relaxing.
   b. crowded.
   c. interesting.

3. The woman took a tour
   a. on a boat.
   b. in a museum.
   c. by herself.

4. The woman thinks art museums are
   a. interesting.
   b. expensive.
   c. boring.

5. The woman liked
   a. shopping.
   b. going to cafés.
   c. talking to French people.

B 🎧 **Listen. Follow the instructions.**

1. _____

2. _____

3. _____

4. _____

5. _____

Unit 9

A **1.** 🎧 **Listen to the information.**

2. 🎧 **Listen again. Circle the correct answers.**

1. The man is talking about a
   a. reality show.
   b. game show.
   c. talk show.

2. The show began in
   a. 2002.
   b. 2003.
   c. 2004.

3. The families on the show are
   a. famous people.
   b. average people.
   c. rich people.

4. The show is about
   a. clothes.
   b. gardens.
   c. houses.

5. The projects are finished in
   a. seven days.
   b. several weeks.
   c. four months.

B 🎧 **Listen. Check (✓) yes or no. Then write your answers.**

	yes	no	
1.	☐	☐	_____
2.	☐	☐	_____
3.	☐	☐	_____
4.	☐	☐	_____
5.	☐	☐	_____

Unit 10

A 1. 🎧 Listen to the conversation.

2. 🎧 Listen again. Circle the correct answers.

1. The woman wants to go
   a. downtown.
   b. to a hotel.
   c. to the park.

2. She is at
   a. the airport.
   b. a bus station.
   c. a department store.

3. The man tells her about
   a. the taxi and the bus.
   b. the subway and the cable car.
   c. the taxi and the subway.

4. The woman will pay
   a. $1.15.
   b. $1.25.
   c. $1.75.

5. The woman is going to take
   a. bus number 1.
   b. bus number 3.
   c. bus number 4.

B 🎧 Listen. Check (✓) your answers. Write more information as needed.

1. ☐ by bus   ☐ on foot _____

2. ☐ by subway   ☐ by car _____

3. ☐ by train   ☐ by taxi _____

4. ☐ BART   ☐ cable car _____

5. ☐ bus   ☐ subway _____

Unit 11

A **1.** 🎧 Listen to the information.

2. 🎧 Listen again. Circle the correct answers.

1. The woman is talking about
   a. an electronics company.
   b. an automobile company.
   c. a computer company.

2. The company is
   a. American.
   b. Korean.
   c. Japanese.

3. The company was known in the U.S. for
   a. expensive products.
   b. unusual products.
   c. lower-priced products.

4. To sell in the U.S., the company
   a. created a new brand.
   b. created new products.
   c. lowered the price.

5. Americans
   a. didn't change their thinking.
   b. bought the products.
   c. didn't buy the products.

B 🎧 Listen. Check (✓) your answers. Write more information as needed.

1. ☐ Japan   ☐ the U.S. _____

2. ☐ candy   ☐ clothing _____

3. ☐ leather shoes   ☐ tea _____

4. ☐ cars   ☐ electronics _____

5. ☐ food   ☐ clothing _____

Unit 12

A 1. 🎧 **Listen to the conversation.**

2. 🎧 **Listen again. Circle the correct answers.**

1. Earth Day is
   a. April 2nd.
   b. April 22nd.
   c. April 12th.

2. The man
   a. knew about Earth Day.
   b. didn't know about Earth Day.
   c. thought Earth Day was a bad idea.

3. On Earth Day, people
   a. do things to help the environment.
   b. celebrate the earth's birthday.
   c. don't use any water.

4. The woman is going to save
   a. water and electricity.
   b. trees and gasoline.
   c. water and gasoline.

5. The man is going to buy
   a. the woman's car.
   b. a bus pass.
   c. a new car.

B 🎧 **Listen. Check (✓) yes or no. Then write your answers.**

	yes	no	
1.	☐	☐	_____
2.	☐	☐	_____
3.	☐	☐	_____
4.	☐	☐	_____
5.	☐	☐	_____

Unit 13

A **1.** 🎧 Listen to the conversation.

2. 🎧 Listen again. Circle the correct answers.

1. The people are
   a. a doctor and a patient.
   b. brother and sister.
   c. two friends. ✓

2. The people are
   a. at a relative's house.
   b. outside a store.
   c. at the park. ✓

3. Andy exercises because he wants to
   a. have more energy. ✓
   b. feel younger.
   c. look younger.

4. Sarah is
   a. an aromatherapist.
   b. a student.
   c. a massage therapist. ✓

5. Andy will probably
   a. never have a massage.
   b. stop jogging.
   c. try getting a massage. ✓

B 🎧 Listen. Check (✓) *yes* or *no*. Then write your answers.

	yes	no	
1.	☐	☐	_____
2.	☐	☐	_____
3.	☐	☐	_____
4.	☐	☐	_____
5.	☐	☐	_____

Unit 14

A **1.** 🎧 **Listen to the conversation.**

2. 🎧 **Listen again. Circle the correct answers.**

1. The people are
   a. business owners.
   b. office workers.
   c. university students.

2. The woman is going to
   a. teach a class.
   b. take a class.
   c. read some books.

3. The woman is
   a. adventurous.
   b. competitive.
   c. ambitious.

4. The man is
   a. sociable.
   b. easygoing.
   c. dependable.

5. The man is also
   a. adventurous.
   b. competitive.
   c. forgetful.

B 🎧 **Listen. Check (✓) your answers. Write more information as needed.**

1. ☐ more adventurous   ☐ less adventurous

   name _____

2. ☐ taking a test   ☐ playing sports

   another situation _____

3. ☐ a big party   ☐ a small party

   another situation _____

4. ☐ draw   ☐ sing

   something else _____

5. ☐ more ambitious   ☐ more easygoing

   another word _____

Unit 15

A **1.** 🎧 Listen to the information.

2. 🎧 Listen again. Circle the correct answers.

1. The celebration is from
   a. Australia.
   b. New Zealand.
   c. Australia and New Zealand.

2. The celebration happens when someone
   a. turns 18.
   b. turns 21.
   c. graduates from high school.

3. People celebrate with
   a. a big party.
   b. a big dance.
   c. a special trip.

4. The person celebrating receives
   a. presents.
   b. advice.
   c. money.

5. The man thinks the celebration
   a. means he is an adult.
   b. isn't important.
   c. has no special meaning but is fun.

B 🎧 Listen. Check (✓) *yes* or *no*. Then write your answers.

	yes	no	
1.	☐	☐	_____
2.	☐	☐	_____
3.	☐	☐	_____
4.	☐	☐	_____
5.	☐	☐	_____

Unit 16

A 1. 🎧 **Listen to the conversation.**

2. 🎧 **Listen again. Circle the correct answers.**

1. The man had the dream
   a. a week ago.
   b. last night.
   c. two days ago.

2. In his dream, he was getting ready for
   a. school.
   b. work.
   c. a trip.

3. He dreamed that
   a. he was wearing pajamas.
   b. his clothes were dirty.
   c. he forgot to eat breakfast.

4. In his dream, the man felt
   a. frightened.
   b. unhappy.
   c. embarrassed.

5. The dream meant
   a. he didn't like school.
   b. he was stressed out.
   c. he forgot something.

B 🎧 **Listen to the dream. Imagine the scene. Then listen again. Write the missing words on the lines.**

I had a (strange) dream last _night_ . I _____ I was in

a (_____) _____ . I was wearing (_____) and

(_____) . _____ , I saw (_____) . He was

(_____) . When he saw me, he _____ to me

and said, (" _____ .")

C 🎧 **Listen again. When you hear the bell, write any word in the circle that makes sense. You can choose any word you want.**

Self-study answer key

Unit 1

Exercise A

1. b
2. a
3. a
4. c
5. b

Unit 2

Exercise A

1. c
2. b
3. c
4. a
5. a

Unit 3

Exercise A

1. c
2. c
3. b
4. a
5. c

Unit 4

Exercise A

1. a
2. b
3. a
4. a
5. c

Unit 5

Exercise A

1. a
2. a
3. b
4. c
5. a

Exercise B

Man should have short, dark, curly hair with a beard and glasses. Woman should have long, straight hair with eyes labeled "green."

Unit 6

Exercise A

1. c
2. a
3. b
4. c
5. c

Unit 7

Exercise A

1. b
2. a
3. b
4. c
5. a

Exercise B

1. sandwich
2. pasta
3. fish
4. shumai
5. potatoes

Unit 8

Exercise A

1. b
2. c
3. a
4. c
5. b

Unit 9
Exercise A
1. a
2. c
3. b
4. c
5. a

Unit 10
Exercise A
1. b
2. a
3. a
4. c
5. c

Unit 11
Exercise A
1. b
2. c
3. c
4. a
5. b

Unit 12
Exercise A
1. b
2. b
3. a
4. c
5. b

Unit 13
Exercise A
1. c
2. c
3. a
4. b
5. c

Unit 14
Exercise A
1. c
2. b
3. c
4. b
5. a

Unit 15
Exercise A
1. c
2. b
3. a
4. a
5. c

Unit 16
Exercise A
1. b
2. a
3. a
4. c
5. c

Exercise B
I had a ( ) dream last **night**. I **dreamed** I was in a ( ) **place**. I was wearing ( ) and ( ). **Suddenly**, I saw ( ). He was ( ). When he saw me, he **spoke** to me and said, (" .")

Self-study track listing

The audio CD contains the Self-study audio exercises from Student's Book 2.

Track	Unit	Page
Track 1	Unit 1	Page 84
Track 2	Unit 2	Page 85
Track 3	Unit 3	Page 86
Track 4	Unit 4	Page 87
Track 5	Unit 5	Page 88
Track 6	Unit 6	Page 89
Track 7	Unit 7	Page 90
Track 8	Unit 8	Page 91
Track 9	Unit 9	Page 92
Track 10	Unit 10	Page 93
Track 11	Unit 11	Page 94
Track 12	Unit 12	Page 95
Track 13	Unit 13	Page 96
Track 14	Unit 14	Page 97
Track 15	Unit 15	Page 98
Track 16	Unit 16	Page 99